First World War
and Army of Occupation
War Diary
France, Belgium and Germany

29 DIVISION
86 Infantry Brigade,
Brigade Trench Mortar Battery
1 July 1916 - 31 July 1916

WO95/2302/7

The Naval & Military Press Ltd
www.nmarchive.com
Published in association with The National Archives

Published by

The Naval & Military Press Ltd

Unit 10 Ridgewood Industrial Park,

Uckfield, East Sussex,

TN22 5QE England

Tel: +44 (0) 1825 749494

www.naval-military-press.com

www.nmarchive.com

This diary has been reprinted in facsimile from the original. Any imperfections are inevitably reproduced and the quality may fall short of modern type and cartographic standards.

© **Crown Copyright**
Images reproduced by permission of The National Archives, London, England, 2015.

Contents

Document type	Place/Title	Date From	Date To
Heading	WO95/2302/7		
Heading	29th Division 86th Infantry Brigade. 86th Brigade Light Trench Mortar Battery July 1916		
War Diary	Auchonvillers	01/07/1916	31/07/1916

WO95/23027

29th Division.
86th Infantry Brigade.

86th BRIGADE

LIGHT TRENCH MORTAR BATTERY

JULY 1 9 1 6

86th Trench Mortar Battery

Vol 1

Army Form C. 2118.

WAR DIARY
or
INTELLIGENCE SUMMARY.
(Erase heading not required.)

Place	Date	Hour	Summary of Events and Information	Remarks and references to Appendices
Acheux-Ville	1st July 1916		The Battery marched to position Acheux Wood & the sig R.- of 3D & inst.	
			No 1 Section took up its position in Sunken Road by end of Sap VII	
			No 2 " " " " proceeded to the dug out - Jacob's Alley	
			No 3 " " " " " " Wilson Craft	
			No 4 " " " " " " 88th Trench	
			No 7 Sec between the lewis of arrived 2400, & 500 per min to reinf. the guns & the Shell carriers to get a charge ammunition by day	
			[See VII]	
			No II Sec. Proceeded to change from cartridges for Red tail latter punt having been received.	
			No III & Sec. drew the guns from Tarnnauillers from the W.edge Jacobs Cut.	
			No IV. in Full ammunition to Carriers.	

WAR DIARY
or
INTELLIGENCE SUMMARY.

(Erase heading not required.)

Army Form C. 2118.

Place	Date	Hour	Summary of Events and Information	Remarks and references to Appendices
	1916 1st July		The method of carrying ammunition adopted was to place 3 complete drills into each sandbag. The necks of the sandbags were then tied together & then very strongly on the shoulder of each carrier. Thus each Carrier had 6 shells. The great difficulty of carrying forward ammunition under fire was decided by carrying two carriers. The weight was far too great & two carriers advanced far to the majority being hit, even our own wire.	

WAR DIARY
or
INTELLIGENCE SUMMARY
(Erase heading not required.)

Army Form C. 2118.

Place	Date	Hour	Summary of Events and Information	Remarks and references to Appendices
Auchonvillers	July 1		Strength of Battery going to action.	
			No 1 Sec. with four guns. 2 Officers + 21 NCOs + men (Capt. Rotter 2 Lt R[?]) (Lt MacDonell Lt H Pollock)	
			No 2 Sec. " " " 2 " + 23 "	
			No 3½ " " 2 guns 1 Sgt in charge + 10 NCOs + men	
			No 4 " " " " " " "	
			During the night of the 30th a heavy bombardment was in progress keeping villages alight 0580 returning until after the assault.	
			At 0720 a mine was exploded under the Hawthorne Redoubt being the signal for No 1 Section to open rapid fire for 10 minutes (this was carried out & 2nd Belt being filled when each gun on to Beaumont-Post-Sector. No 1 Section immediately took debris last falling hurled over to the rear lit of the crater) the officer in charge 1st MacDonnell was killed on the was expended. The Officer in charge 1st MacDonnell was killed on the advance to the Crater, 4th bombardment & to Pollock was wounded in the arm	

Place	Date	Hour	Summary of Events and Information	Remarks and references to Appendices
Auchonvillers	1st July		No III ½ Sec. who were unattached to the Middlesex Regt. The gun to C. Coy & 1 gun to D. Coy. That sec't. put up ladders & Bally Alley & took 1 gun under Colsted Martin both up ladders. Du. the right of the Crater with first Coy & the other gun under Corpor'l Baker both up from the position between the Crater & the Sunken Road afterwards joining No 1 Section in the Sunken Road. No IV ½ Sec. who were attached to the R.D.F. started to the Advance & proceeded along the Crawler in rear of the Z Coy & till Seuis's gun section's when they were held up, eventually arriving at the Trapego Sap & remaining in tealison to Goers for some time they were sent back to S8 Trench. The assault having failed No I Section remained in the Sunken road in defensive positions, eleven transversed two & a fire on the German trenches the survivors of the remaining Section along our trenches. At 1900 No I Section was relieved & the both eps afterwards Sea. dielos along the Brigade front.	

Army Form C. 2118.

WAR DIARY
or
INTELLIGENCE SUMMARY.
(Erase heading not required.)

Place	Date	Hour	Summary of Events and Information	Remarks and references to Appendices
Authuille	July 1		The following casualties occurred during the assault.	
			Lt. D. Rae D. Campbell killed 2/Lt Pollith wounded	
			274/86 Pte Berlin P. " 4912 Cpl Clark W. "	
			1812 " Cumming J. " 2281 " Bryson W. "	
			3041 " Lilly J. " 2144 L/Cpl Pelletier J. "	
			646 Pte Bolton J. missing	
			1643 " Bleiloch G. "	
			23319 " Erskine and 6 Dundas	
			613 " Greenwood J. "	
			2326 J " Kesler J. "	
			22114 " Macnair P. "	
			23022 " Ridge R. "	
			16429 " Pitt E. "	
			467 J " Larking W. W. "	
			3905 " Clark J. "	
			442 Northshaw J. missing	

WAR DIARY
or
INTELLIGENCE SUMMARY.

Army Form C. 2118.

Place	Date	Hour	Summary of Events and Information	Remarks and references to Appendices
Auchonvillers	July 4	4	On the 4th inst. the Battery was relieved by the 10th Bde T.A.B. proceeded to Bruailly Noeux to return to 6.	
		8	On the night of the 8/9th the Battery took over from the 89th Bde T.A.R.B. in the sub-sect of the line from the Mary Redan to the Ancre.	
		12	I found no emplacements constructed to accommodate gun pits & being complete on the night of the 12th, about the Bell Pit(?).	
		16	My pits were dug during the period being constructed in corrected with each pit.	
		20	On the night of the 20th with H. Greene I took a recced of material from Bray ale, & jump'd into the ravine below the rest firing line. I could see on a moonlight night had been causing a deal of trouble. He shells appeared to have considerable effect. On the right of the (?) my new emplacement in W of Ravine	

T2134. Wt. W708—776. 500'000. 4/15. Sir J.C. & S.

WAR DIARY or INTELLIGENCE SUMMARY.

Army Form C. 2118.

Place	Date	Hour	Summary of Events and Information	Remarks and references to Appendices
Authuille	July 20		Trench received a number of direct hits from heavy shells, the gun pit which had six feet of overhead cover was completely wrecked & the gun considerably damaged. The Vicars were set to work destroying the trench which erupted input.	
	28		On the 27th & 28th the Battery were relieved by the 9th, 2nd B Worcesters & sectn to Mailly Maillet & thence to Battery to Beaumont & then to the 29th & 30th moving the Battery wireless to Bonval to Ulb. arriving at 1900.	
	29		At 08.00 the Battery marched to Louvillers arriving at entrained for Beauvais - Ecuisseau, arriving at 1910, arriving at Our Abbile at 2000.	
	30		Left Mondicourt 0630 arriving Camp C. 1300.	
	31		Parade - Kit + Rifle inspection.	

J Mathew Capt
O.C. 86 TM Bty
1 OC 86 TM Bty